THE ULTIMATE WOULD YOU RATHER BOOK FOR COUPLES

LovityNote
The Ultimate Would You Rather Book for Couples

www.lovitynote.com

Images by Tupungato/stock.adobe.com, Yanka/stock.adobe.com, Rudzhan/stock.adobe.com, 123levit/stock.adobe.com, Paolo/stock.adobe.com, mahaputrarahadian11/stock.adobe.com

First published by LovityNote in Germany in 2025
First printed January 2025

9783949676550
First Edition

Contents

Introduction

Welcome to *The Ultimate Would You Rather Book for Couples*! Inside, you'll find 250 fun, thought-provoking, and sometimes delightfully challenging questions designed to bring you closer, spark laughter, and inspire deeper conversations.

With these questions, you'll not only uncover your partner's preferences and hidden dreams but also reflect on meaningful topics together. It's a unique way to learn more about each other, and even about yourself, while building stronger connections and creating lasting memories.

This book offers countless hours of genuine fun, whether you're on a date night, a road trip, unwinding before bed, or simply looking for something lighthearted to do together. Every question is an invitation to step into a moment of joy, curiosity, and connection.

So grab your favorite snacks, cozy up, and let the questions lead you on a journey of laughter, discovery, and love.

How to Use This Book

This book is designed to help you and your partner have fun and deepen your bond through carefully curated questions divided into 10 sections. Feel free to explore them in any order and setting that feels right for you.

Some questions are quick and playful, perfect for a burst of fun, while others invite you to pause and reflect together. No matter the tone, every question serves as a starting point for meaningful conversations and shared moments of joy. You can use the questions as casual conversation starters or, for a more competitive twist, turn them into a game with a chance to win prizes along the way!

If you decide to play, here's how it works:
Partner A can use the space to the left of the white dot at the bottom of each question card to write down their answers or comments. Partner B can use the space to the right.

At the end of each section, you'll find a prize suggestion for the winner and an end-of-round reflection question to keep the conversation flowing. To add even more fun, here are three suggested games you can play, or feel free to create your own rules as long as you're having fun together!

Guess the Answer

Partner A reads a question aloud and writes down what they think Partner B's answer will be. Then, Partner B shares their answer. If Partner A guessed correctly, they earn 1 point. Keep track of your points on the provided space or a separate piece of paper. Switch roles for the next question. At the end of the section, tally up your points to declare the winner!

Say the Word

Partner A reads a question aloud and, before Partner B answers, they write down one word (a noun) they think will appear in Partner B's response. Partner B then answers. If Partner A's word appears, they earn 1 point. Remember: the guessed word cannot be one mentioned in the question. To avoid mix-ups, you can record your answers as audio and review them if needed. Keep track of points and total them at the end of the section.

Make Your Case

Both partners answer each question with a twist! After hearing the question, take one minute to think and jot down reasons for your answer. The partner with the most reasons earns 1 point. If you both have the same number of reasons, decide who wins based on creativity or strength of arguments. Add up your points at the end of the section to see who wins.

Notes:

- For *Guess the Answer* and *Say the Word*, you can alternate who answers each question or both answer every question, taking turns asking and guessing.
- In the event of a tie at the end of a section, both partners win the same prize.
- These games can also be played with multiple couples! Simply skip the prizes and use a sheet of paper to write down answers and points for each couple.

Whether you're playing for points or simply diving into the questions for fun, this book is your invitation to strengthen your connection, one question at a time. So grab a pen, settle in with your partner, and let the games (and conversations) begin!

SECTION 1

HOW TO USE THIS BOOK

Playful Dilemmas

Would you rather

A share a passionate kiss with your partner every time you walk past a fountain

or

B sing your favorite song together every time you wait in line?

Would you rather

A crack the puzzles of a tricky escape room with your partner

or

B lead separate teams in a fun, competitive treasure hunt?

Would you rather

A your partner be a rock star

or

B a Nobel Prize–winning scientist?

Would you rather

A have your partner wear a blindfold while feeding you

or

B while picking out your clothes and dressing you?

Would you rather

A watch the Northern Lights or

or

B take part in the world's biggest lantern festival?

Would you rather

A own a custom-made hot air balloon for romantic adventures with your partner

or

B a personalized treehouse built just for the two of you?

Would you rather

A dress up as Beauty and the Beast

or

B Romeo and Juliet for a costume party with your partner?

Would you rather

A wear your partner's fragrance for a week

or

B their underwear for a day?

Would you rather

A start your day feeding each other breakfast like affectionate lovebirds

or

B end your night grooming each other (picking lint from pajamas and fixing hair) like playful chimpanzees?

Would you rather

A eat soup with a fork

or

B drink water from a soup plate?

Would you rather

A climb a mountain with your partner to enjoy breathtaking views

or

B dive underwater together to explore vibrant marine life?

Would you rather

A go on a super fun date with your partner once a week

or

B have intimate physical connection daily?

Would you rather

A type messages with a stylus held in your mouth

or

B open the fridge using only your feet?

Would you rather

A always bathe with citrus-scented soap

or

B make your own bubble-gum-flavored toothpaste for life?

Would you rather

A develop a secret code with your partner using quirky animal sounds

or

B invent a private language of 50 made-up words?

Would you rather

A have a marshmallow-themed date night (roasting, dipping in fondue, and tossing marshmallows like pros)

or

B enjoy a cozy board game night at home?

Would you rather

A go on a romantic vacation in a glass capsule house suspended in the air with stunning views

or

B stay in a high-tech hotel room with customizable LED walls to design your perfect ambiance?

Would you rather

A have tantric sex with your partner

or

B engage in role-playing?

Would you rather

A sing everything you say to your partner

or

B whisper every word into their ear?

Would you rather

A swap daily routines with your partner for a week

or

B switch bodies for a day?

Would you rather

A have a sticky-feather pillow fight with your partner in the house

or

B a stinky water balloon fight outside?

Would you rather

A gently touch noses with your partner like penguins before sharing a kiss

or

B do a playful cat-like head bump before locking lips?

Would you rather

A spend a week with your partner without talking

or

B without touching?

Would you rather

A take ice skating lessons with your partner

or

B start horseback riding classes together?

Winner

The Better Half:

Love Points:

Prize

Your partner will set up a luxurious candlelit bath with calming scents and your favorite drink and snacks for the ultimate relaxation.

Reflection

Did any of your partner's answers reveal something surprising or new about them? If so, what was it?

SECTION 2
SECTION 1

Sweet & Silly

Would you rather

A swap bed sides

or

B smartphones with your partner?

Would you rather

A sleep in socks every night

or

B sleep only in your underwear year-round?

Would you rather

A go on a nostalgic date in each other's childhood neighborhood

or

B spend the evening watching your favorite cartoons together?

Would you rather

A try to seduce your partner by strutting like a peacock with an imaginary tail

or

B by doing a high-energy dance like a bird-of-paradise?

Would you rather

A sing a lullaby to help your partner sleep

or

B gently stroke their head until they drift off?

Would you rather

A talk to your partner as if they were royalty

or

B as if they were a baby?

Would you rather

A greet people with a backflip

or

B say goodbye by thumping your chest like a gorilla?

Would you rather

A have your partner's eyebrows

or

B their fingernails?

Would you rather

A know how to tap-dance

or

B how to yodel?

Would you rather

A mow the lawn wearing a clown wig

or

B take out the trash doing a victory dance?

Would you rather

A visit a fortune teller

or

B consult an astrologer?

Would you rather

A spend an evening hula-hooping

or

B jumping rope with your partner?

Would you rather

A go on a surprise vacation planned by your partner

or

B plan one for them?

Would you rather

A swim with dolphins

or

B ride camels with your partner?

Would you rather

A have your partner dress up as a police officer

or

B as a superhero for a spicy date night with you?

Would you rather

A have different hair lengths

or

B two distinct hair colors on each side of your head?

Would you rather

A stay up past midnight having deep conversations with your partner

or

B wake up early to watch the sunrise together?

Would you rather

A always dress in matching outfits with your partner

or

B never know what the other will wear on your outings together?

Would you rather

A sneeze every time your partner says "I love you"

or

B get the hiccups for five minutes every time you eat a meal they prepare?

Would you rather

A pose as living mannequins in a store window with your partner

or

B run a lemonade stand together at a local festival?

Would you rather

A have chicken legs

or

B orangutan arms?

Would you rather

A clap whenever someone says “hi”

or

B giggle every time you hear your name?

Would you rather

A have hair growing out of your ears

or

B a dark hair sprout on your nose every day?

Would you rather

A fall asleep in a hammock with your partner under the stars

or

B cuddle in a cozy fort you built together indoors?

Winner

The Better Half:

____

Love Points:

____

Prize

Your partner must either sing you a lullaby or gently stroke your head until you fall asleep—whichever you choose.

Reflection

Which one of your partner's answers was the most unexpected to you, and why?

SECTION 3
SECTION 2

The Great Debate

Would you rather

A meet your partner's favorite celebrity

or

B have them meet yours and chat on your behalf?

Would you rather

A blow a kiss to a stranger at a crosswalk

or

B wink at your dentist while they're checking your teeth?

Would you rather

A post 10 photos of you and your partner a day on social media

or

B never share anything about your relationship online?

Would you rather

A have three-day weekends

or

B five extra hours each day to spend however you like?

Would you rather

A have your partner throw you a surprise party that's not quite your style

or

B stick to a safe dinner date?

Would you rather

A have a mirror

or

B a TV on your bedroom ceiling?

Would you rather

A visit Buckingham Palace as an honored guest

or

B be named Citizen of the Year?

Would you rather

A change your name to one chosen by 100 strangers

or

B to your partner's favorite unisex name?

Would you rather

A start a bakery business with your partner

or

B run a yoga studio together?

Would you rather

A perform a duet with your partner as the opening act for a sold-out concert

or

B do a stand-up comedy show together?

Would you rather

A live out the most romantic scene from your favorite movie with your partner

or

B see your love story turned into a movie?

Would you rather

A party like teenagers with your partner

or

B have deep conversations like old souls?

Would you rather

A dine out for the rest of your life but never get to choose the menu

or

B only eat home-cooked meals that you prepare yourself?

Would you rather

A give yourself a haircut

or

B trust your partner to do it?

Would you rather

A explore space on a one-way shuttle leaving Earth forever

or

B remain behind after humanity migrates to other planets?

Would you rather

A debate a controversial topic live on television with one hour to prepare

or

B interview the president with only 15 minutes to prepare?

Would you rather

A never need sleep

or

B never need food?

Would you rather

A live in a world without insects

or

B without reptiles?

Would you rather

A have your own town with your partner

or

B have your own word in the dictionary?

Would you rather

A uncover humanity's origins

or

B its destiny?

Would you rather

A start a podcast with your partner about your life

or

B try to become travel influencers as a couple?

Would you rather

A relive the most wonderful moment you shared with your partner

or

B forget your most awkward one together?

Would you rather

A co-write a Hollywood script with your partner

or

B release an album together?

Would you rather

A adopt a pet with your partner

or

B spend your weekends volunteering at an animal shelter together?

Winner

The Better Half:

Love Points:

Prize

You get to be the stylist, director, and photographer for a photoshoot featuring your partner. Whatever the theme (high fashion, action hero, or total goofball) capture their best or funniest angles!

Reflection

Which of your partner's answers made you feel most connected to them, and why?

SECTION 4
SECTION 3

This or That?

Would you rather

A invite friends over for a disco party

or

B host a poker night?

Would you rather

A choose your partner's wedding attire

or

B let them choose yours?

Would you rather

A listen exclusively to your partner's playlists

or

B eat only their favorite snacks?

Would you rather

A join a reality show for couples

or

B compete on a trivia game show together?

Would you rather

A go on a casino night date

or

B spend a full day at a water park with your partner?

Would you rather

A drive a car shaped like a bathtub

or

B one covered in your photos?

Would you rather

A never win anything in your life

or

B never get scammed?

Would you rather

A have a pet lizard your partner loves

or

B a pet dog they hate?

Would you rather

A start a book club

or

B participate in chess tournaments?

Would you rather

A drive the world's most expensive car

or

B wear the most luxurious outfit?

Would you rather

A wake up to a defensive red fox in your bed

or

B try to sleep in a noisy barn full of restless horses?

Would you rather

A see your partner in cute bunny pajamas

or

B classy satin pajamas?

Would you rather

A give up chocolate bars

or

B chips?

Would you rather

A always feel a bit cold

or

B always feel a bit hot?

Would you rather

A walk a fashion runway

or

B have your designs showcased at a fashion show?

Would you rather

A give up hot beverages

or

B bread?

Would you rather

A go canyoning

or

B bungee jumping with your partner?

Would you rather

A find out your partner collects dried ladybugs

or

B antique keys?

Would you rather

A spend a weekend in a tiny house in the valley

or

B on a houseboat down the river?

Would you rather

A go on a Mediterranean cruise

or

B take a motorbike trip through Europe?

Would you rather

A have shaky hands

or

B sweaty feet?

Would you rather

A have a lifetime supply of electronic gadgets

or

B clothing items?

Would you rather

A eat your food cold

or

B overcooked?

Would you rather

A receive compliments about your intelligence

or

B your looks?

Winner

The Better Half:

Love Points:

Prize

Your partner must write two compliments about your intelligence and two about your looks. You get to read one per day.

Reflection

Was there a question in this section that inspired you to set a goal as a couple or plan a new experience together?

SECTION 5
SECTION 4

Pick Your Poison

Would you rather

A be unable to pronounce the first letter of your partner's name in any word

or

B have to end every sentence with the first syllable of their name?

Would you rather

A lose all your memories with your partner

or

B never make new ones together?

Would you rather

A have your partner know all your embarrassing childhood moments

or

B all your secret fantasies?

Would you rather

A have your partner fall asleep during an intimate moment

or

B hear them chuckle instead?

Would you rather

A eat a meal prepared by a child

or

B by someone who strongly dislikes you?

Would you rather

A attend a job interview while dealing with loud stomach growls

or

B with crusty eyes?

Would you rather

A listen to the sound of styrofoam rubbing against styrofoam

or

B a fork scraping against a plate?

Would you rather

A enter a government office doing a cartwheel

or

B loudly exclaim “Finally!” at the end of a business meeting?

Would you rather

A have the alphabet tattooed around your neck

or

B always have the tip of your big toenail as long as your eyelashes?

Would you rather

A eat honey made by bees raised next to a dumpster

or

B ice cream made with pig milk?

Would you rather

A always feel hungry

or

B always feel overfull no matter how much you eat?

Would you rather

A accidentally send an inappropriate email to your boss that was meant for your partner

or

B have your colleagues discover you badmouthed them?

Would you rather

A live near a rooster that crows at dawn

or

B next to a busy BBQ restaurant?

Would you rather

A have all your digital photos accidentally shared online

or

B erased forever?

Would you rather

A live in a house with no curtains

or

B one without bathroom doors?

Would you rather

A try fried tarantulas

or

B eat raw tuna eyeballs?

Would you rather

A taste wine made by grape-stomping

or

B try blood sausage?

Would you rather

A eat food that smells like perfume

or

B wear perfume that smells like food?

Would you rather

A be missing a side tooth

or

B have no eyebrows at all?

Would you rather

A have a constantly runny nose

or

B a teary eye that never stops?

Would you rather

A not call or message anyone for two weeks

or

B not listen to any music for two months?

Would you rather

A step in dog poop

or

B get sprinkled by sloth pee?

Would you rather

A go a week without washing your hands

or

B without washing your face?

Would you rather

A sit for hours in the rain

or

B seek shelter in a pigpen?

Winner

The Better Half:

____

Love Points:

____

Prize

You get to choose a movie scene that your partner must rehearse and perform in front of you to the best of their ability. Take full advantage and be creative!

Reflection

Which one of your answers in this section would be the most challenging for you if it came true, and why?

SECTION 6
SECTION 5

No Easy Way Out

Would you rather

A share a toothbrush

or

B a razor with your partner?

Would you rather

A spend a romantic weekend in a cold countryside home with no heat

or

B with nothing but strawberries to eat?

Would you rather

A have toilet paper hanging from your pants in front of coworkers

or

B visible boogers in your nose while on a date with your partner?

Would you rather

A accidentally livestream an argument with your partner

or

B be caught gossiping about friends?

Would you rather

A wash your hair with dish soap

or

B use hand cream as a face moisturizer?

Would you rather

A sit on a strange-smelling, damp bus seat

or

B have a stranger's gum stuck in your hair?

Would you rather

A never visit your hometown again

or

B never go to the beach again?

Would you rather

A taste dry dog food

or

B chew on playdough?

Would you rather

A stick your arm in a bucket of mud

or

B pet a friendly rat?

Would you rather

A never make new friends again

or

B never listen to a new song again?

Would you rather

A drink a cocktail sweeter than sugar

or

B one sour as vinegar?

Would you rather

A give up using washing machines

or

B all hot water in your home?

Would you rather

A never speak your native language again

or

B never look at old pictures of yourself?

Would you rather

A give up all your hobbies

or

B give up your phone?

Would you rather

A be stuck in an elevator with your partner

or

B lost in the woods together?

Would you rather

A go on a 10-day tech-free meditation retreat for couples

or

B do a 10-day raw vegetable detox together?

Would you rather

A eat a spoonful of mayonnaise

or

B drink a cup of pickle juice?

Would you rather

A eat food that's been on the ground for a second

or

B swim in a pond full of moss?

Would you rather

A wear sandals with socks all year long

or

B wear swimming goggles everywhere you go for a week?

Would you rather

A message your partner using only emojis

or

B communicate only through song lyrics?

Would you rather

A cuddle a hedgehog while you sleep

or

B have a stinky badger in a cage beside your bed all night?

Would you rather

A sleep in the bathtub

or

B take a shower in the sink?

Would you rather

A wear a Halloween hat all year round

or

B always have to wear cowboy boots?

Would you rather

A address everyone as "Hey, you!"

or

B thank everyone by bowing down?

Winner

The Better Half:

____

Love Points:

____

Prize

Your partner must write either a mini story or a poem inspired by you, highlighting your best attributes.

Reflection

Which question in this section led to the funniest answer, and what made it so amusing?

SECTION 7
SECTION 6

Choose Your Fate

Would you rather

A give up foreplay

or

B never be able to hug your partner again?

Would you rather

A have five children

or

B five pets?

Would you rather

A have the police mistakenly search your house causing chaos

or

B be falsely arrested and spend a day in jail?

Would you rather

A live next to a nosy neighbor who watches your every move

or

B receive mysterious packages from an unknown sender every week?

Would you rather

A your partner snore

or

B kick in their sleep?

Would you rather

A always wear a pirate's eye patch on one eye

or

B have a pirate's hook attached to your arm?

Would you rather

A dine like an aristocrat all the time

or

B always eat meals as fast as possible?

Would you rather

A eat the same breakfast every day

or

B read the same book every night?

Would you rather

A have telescopic vision

or

B night vision?

Would you rather

A spend two hours waiting for someone to pick you up in cold, snowy weather

or

B be stuck in a broken car on a hot day?

Would you rather

A lose the ability to see colors

or

B the ability to hear anything except human voices?

Would you rather

A study one hour daily for life

or

B master a new skill every month?

Would you rather

A grow your own food

or

B craft your own furniture?

Would you rather

A forget all the memories you've made with your partner

or

B lose the ability to create new ones together?

Would you rather

A show up at a wedding with your partner looking so fabulous that you both outshine the couple

or

B arrive underdressed and stand out for being too casual?

Would you rather

A survive an alien abduction

or

B a comet impact?

Would you rather

A spend 24 hours on a deserted island

or

B in a supposedly haunted mansion?

Would you rather

A never smell flowers again

or

B never smell the rain?

Would you rather

A let your partner choose every movie you watch

or

B every restaurant you visit?

Would you rather

A your partner tickle you until you cry from laughing

or

B playfully chase you until you're out of breath?

Would you rather

A have to run everywhere you go

or

B crawl to get around your house?

Would you rather

A drink with your lips half-open

or

B sleep with your eyes half-closed?

Would you rather

A always be running late

or

B always be stood up?

Would you rather

A always wear shoes that make a squeaky sound when you walk

or

B always wear mismatched socks?

Winner

The Better Half:

____

Love Points:

____

Prize

Your partner must wear either a pirate's eye patch on one eye or a pirate's hook on their arm for a full day at home—whichever they choose.

Reflection

Which question in this section was the most difficult for you to answer, and what made it challenging?

SECTION 8
SECTION 7

Stuck in the Middle

Would you rather

A take your partner to meet your favorite high school teachers

or

B to your class reunion?

Would you rather

A give up your favorite food forever

or

B have it for dinner every single day?

Would you rather

A race your partner in a go-kart showdown

or

B team up for a basketball match with mutual friends?

Would you rather

A take salsa classes with your partner for fun

or

B learn professional-level cooking to show off your culinary skills in couple cook-offs?

Would you rather

A witness your worst enemy embarrass themselves

or

B leave them awestruck by your achievements?

Would you rather

A live life to the fullest spending every penny on enjoyment

or

B cut all leisure expenses to grow your bank account?

Would you rather

A inspire a novel about your life

or

B have a famous portrait of you?

Would you rather

A be surrounded by people you admire

or

B people who admire you?

Would you rather

A work for your favorite celebrity and keep it strictly professional

or

B work for someone random and form a strong personal connection?

Would you rather

A never get sick again

or

B never injure yourself again?

Would you rather

A own a Picasso painting

or

B a royal crown?

Would you rather

A have your dream house

or

B your dream job?

Would you rather

A create your own video game

or

B design your own board game?

Would you rather

A have a one-time pass to visit any place in the world

or

B the chance to talk to any one person you choose?

Would you rather

A have a deluxe home cinema

or

B a luxurious wellness spa in your house?

Would you rather

A only have friends who are 10 years younger than you

or

B 10 years older?

Would you rather

A forget your anniversary

or

B have your partner forget it?

Would you rather

A drag yourself to bed at a turtle's pace every night

or

B get ready to start your day at lightning speed every morning?

Would you rather

A be a loved pet in someone's home

or

B a wild animal going on adventures in nature?

Would you rather

A celebrate New Year's Eve on a plane watching fireworks from above

or

B in your yard with dozens of glowing candlelights and party poppers?

Would you rather

A never have bad breath again

or

B never need to pass gas again?

Would you rather

A be the life of the party but have no close friends

or

B have one best friend but no wider social circle?

Would you rather

A cohost a talent show with your partner on national TV

or

B be the judges who pick the winner?

Would you rather

A take a shot at winning $1,000,000 in a professional golf tournament

or

B $1,000 in a local bowling game?

Winner

The Better Half:

____

Love Points:

____

Prize

Your partner will treat you to a luxurious wellness spa experience of your choice, selecting from a one-hour scalp, foot, or neck and back massage.

Reflection

Did you learn or realize something new about yourself while answering these questions? If so, what was it?

SECTION 9
SECTION 8

Moment of Truth

Would you rather

A your partner have a '60s-style wardrobe

or

B always dress in modern sportswear?

Would you rather

A know the answer to any question you ask

or

B be guaranteed lifelong happiness?

Would you rather

A follow Kama Sutra instructions every time you're intimate with your partner

or

B only be intimate outside your home?

Would you rather

A take a two-month staycation

or

B a thrilling weeklong dream trip?

Would you rather

A receive authentic criticism

or

B insincere flattery?

Would you rather

A have a perfectly proportioned body

or

B captivating facial features?

Would you rather

A always be the center of attention

or

B move unnoticed in a crowd?

Would you rather

A dye all your clothes black

or

B add trendy cutouts to them?

Would you rather

A know when people dislike you

or

B when they're jealous of you?

Would you rather

A always receive handmade gifts

or

B always make gifts for everyone?

Would you rather

A hang glide over the Grand Canyon

or

B fly a helicopter above the mist of Niagara Falls?

Would you rather

A have a blueberry-sized birthmark on your face

or

B a mango-sized one on your back?

Would you rather

A have fewer regrets

or

B more accomplishments?

Would you rather

A study biographies of great men

or

B the history of technology?

Would you rather

A have a jacuzzi in your garden

or

B a pool table in your basement?

Would you rather

A be seen as mean

or

B naive?

Would you rather

A go birdwatching in the Amazon

or

B snorkel with blue whales in Sri Lanka?

Would you rather

A be liked

or

B appreciated?

Would you rather

A live an easy, ordinary life

or

B strive for greatness by taking risks?

Would you rather

A have a best friend who cracks jokes all the time

or

B one who's overly serious?

Would you rather

A play the drums but never receive a compliment

or

B play the pan flute and always captivate your audience?

Would you rather

A dress up as Santa for Halloween

or

B have pumpkin decorations for Christmas?

Would you rather

A spend a whole week with your face painted all white

or

B with your hair dyed neon blue?

Would you rather

A gently wake up every morning by a massaging pillow

or

B by a soothingly rocking bed?

Winner

The Better Half:

____

Love Points:

____

Prize

Your partner must go out to a place of your choice—make it funny but keep it nice—dressed in either '60s style or full sportswear.

Reflection

If you had to publicly debate your partner about one of your differing answers, which question would it be, and what would you say?

SECTION 10
SECTION 9

Impossible Scenarios

Would you rather

A travel back in time to hang out with cavemen for a day

or

B see real-life dinosaurs and mammoths?

Would you rather

A have all your dreams recorded to watch later

or

B jump into your partner's dreams anytime?

Would you rather

A live in the past before electricity

or

B in a future where everyone is limited to 100 square feet of living space?

Would you rather

A win $1,000,000 that you must give away to a stranger

or

B win a house in the middle of the ocean that you can't sell or rent?

Would you rather

A live in a world where you can never touch the ground

or

B never be exposed to sunlight?

Would you rather

A watch a documentary featuring all your ancestors from the past 100 years

or

B one about your descendants 100 years into the future?

Would you rather

A be reincarnated as a human

or

B as an intelligent alien species?

Would you rather

A spend a day as a cheetah, feeling the thrill of ultimate speed

or

B as a caterpillar, experiencing the magic of transformation?

Would you rather

A perform invisible internet searches in your mind

or

B foresee the future?

Would you rather

A travel back in time to meet any five people of your choice

or

B tune into the news from any future date you choose?

Would you rather

A instantly teleport to anyone who mentions you, whether positively or negatively,

or

B have people teleport to you whenever you miss them?

Would you rather

A be immortal

or

B live in a world without cruelty?

Would you rather

A live in a world where you must pay a fee every time you leave your house

or

B attend a parenthood college before you can have children?

Would you rather

A relive your 18th year

or

B skip five years into the future?

Would you rather

A meet your partner as a child

or

B as an old person?

Would you rather

A be able to astral project with your partner

or

B telepathically hear what others think about you two as a couple?

Would you rather

A be able to squeeze unnoticed into any tiny space you want

or

B get invited to every exciting event in the world?

Would you rather

A have the skill to paint any vision you have flawlessly

or

B masterfully play any composition you want on the piano?

Would you rather

A wake up one day to discover your entire life was just a dream you could revisit in your sleep

or

B live the same life on an endless loop?

Would you rather

A bring any invention you imagine to life

or

B change any law at will?

Would you rather

A hear people's emotions

or

B feel their thoughts?

Would you rather

A find yourself in a castle beside a battlefield

or

B encounter a hostile ghost in your house?

Would you rather

A have the eyes of a chameleon

or

B the ears of a bat?

Would you rather

A wake up with a different hairstyle

or

B a different smile every day?

Winner

The Better Half:

____

Love Points:

____

Prize

Your partner must create an artwork (a small sketch, painting, or digital design) inspired by an impossible dream you describe. Then, they must print it on a T-shirt and wear it for at least one day.

Reflection

If one answer from this section could magically come true, which one would you choose, and why?

Congratulations!

You've made it to the end.

The Champion

The Ultimate Better Half:

Love Wins:

Made in United States
Troutdale, OR
08/17/2025

33726114R00096